Flashback

Flashback

The story of the North East
1939 - 1985

Northern Heritage Consultancy Ltd.

Tyne Tees Television

Published by Northern Heritage Consultancy Ltd.

20 Great North Road

Jesmond

Newcastle upon Tyne

© Tyne Tees Television and Northern Heritage Consultancy Ltd. 1990

First Published 1990

Art work: G A Williams

Design: Duncan McDonald

Reproduction: V & H Repro, Newcastle

Printed and Bound in England by: Knight-Fletcher Print, Tyne & Wear

ISBN 1 872346 04 9

Contents

Contributors

David Brough, Steve Bradwell, Jonathan Brown, Sheila Browne, Roy Deane, Gordon Lee, John Gwyn, Alex Jacklin, Sue Kennet, David Milne, Alex Murchie, Gillian Robinson, Derek Nelson, Ed Skelding, Charles Slater, Derek Smith, David Thomasson, Peter Winter.

Television Series Producer: **Trevor Hearing**

Historical advisor to the television series: **Dr. Robert Colls**

Acknowledgements

The publisher acknowledges the help and cooperation of Tyne Tees Television in publishing this book. We are indebted to the many people, individuals and organisations who have allowed us to make use of their photographs, a complete list of whom is on page 142. A special thanks must go to the Northern Echo without whose generous assistance this book would not have been possible. The Green Howards, Durham Light Infantry and Royal Northumberland Fusiliers museums have all let us use their time and resources. The Newcastle Journal has kindly allowed us to use headlines from the newspaper. Various local libraries have assisted us greatly Newcastle City Library Local Studies section has given us access to their collection. A special thanks must go to Mrs Helen Bunyan from Middlesbrough Central Library for her perseverance and to Veronica Clauzel for her fortitude during the production stage of the book. At Tyne Tees we would like to thank Peter McArthur, Peter Moth and Jim Manson.

"WE ARE AT WAR"

KING'S CALL TO THE EMPIRE

"STAND CALM, FIRM AND UNITED"

"WE CAN ONLY DO THE RIGHT AS WE SEE IT"

STIRRING SPEECH FROM THE PALACE

Sunday 3rd September 1939. Neville Chamberlain addresses a nation at war.

The stage is set for a People's war.

"This morning the British Ambassador in Berlin handed the German Government a final note stating that unless we heard from them by 11 o'clock that they were prepared at once to withdraw their troops from Poland a state of war would exist between us. I have to tell you that no such undertaking has been received and that consequently this country is at war with Germany."

Tow Law Mobilisation.

Adolf Hitler.

"On September 3rd, I was listening to the radio which announced the war had started. The coming war, a threatened war. You are filled with a boyish enthusiasm as you thought it was something great that was going to happen."
L/Cpl Fred Jameson, 9th RNF 1940/46

Preparing for war in Consett, August 1938.

"The first thing I remember about the war is being presented with a gas mask and I was told to wear it at all times and never to leave it anywhere.

When the sirens went off we were all huddled along to the Anderson shelter...To us it was great fun, all the neighbours came along and we would sing songs about the white cliffs of Dover."

Maureen Raper, schoolgirl

Children leave for the protection of the Countryside.

An evacuee leaves home - Sunderland Station 1939.

Labelled for the Country - Evacuees from London.

The Blitz reaches the North East. German planes started coming over regularly, targeting heavy industry.

Marsh Road, Middlesbrough.

Bank holiday 1942. The Middlesbrough Evening Gazette's chief photographer, Teddy Baxter, is able to capture one of the few shots of its type during the war as he was on the opposite platform when the station was bombed. The photograph was censored until after the war. Seven people were killed, and many injured, during the raid.

*The morning after -
West Hartlepool, 1940.*

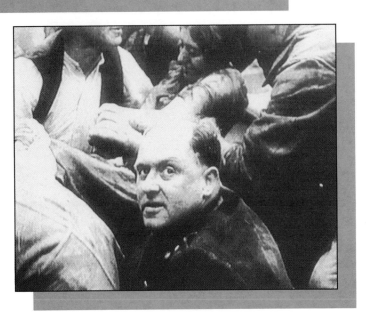

*King Street - North
Shields, 1941.*

"Five inches of water was the amount always to have in the bath to be at the ready. I do remember years later visiting a patient and the water in the bath was slimy green and I said 'what's this in the bath?' and she said 'well I've kept it all the years because we were always told to keep five inches of water.' It had been kept there all that time."

Maureen Raper

Auxiliary Fire Brigade - Neville's Cross, August 1st 1941

Bomb Disposal - Co. Durham, Christmas 1940.

Bomber Command.

"The men of Lindisfarne are mostly fishermen. Those who are not in the forces are in the lobster business...But when they are not catching lobsters, they are homeguarding as the men of Holy Island have always been doing since the first recorded invasion in 793. They also provide a crew for the lifeboat...homeguards and lifeboatmen, a pretty good war effort."

Contemporary Newsreel

"Between the eight of us we'd only one rifle for quite a time and there were no bullets for a long, long time. We did the sloping arms and present arms with brush shafts in the yard. When we got rifles we were limited to four bullets apiece and used to say, 'What happens if you meet five Germans?'"

Ray Carr, Staintondale Home Guard

Home defence - The North's 'Dad's Army' prepares for an expected invasion.

13

1943 Minister of Labour Ernest Bevin conscripts labour to work in the pits.

Sacriston Colliery, 1940.

"We have reached the point at which there are not enough miners to produce the amount of coal needed to keep the war effort going. We need 720,000 men continuously employed in this industry."

Ernest Bevin

A hewer working on a narrow seam - Ashington Colliery.

Young Men Can "Join Up" As Miners

ALL young men who were under 25 when they registered and who become available for service in the Forces can volunteer for work in the mines.

"Preliminaries are much the same as if they were joining the army. A miner's hat is quite as honourable and necessary as a soldier's hat. These boys drawn from all classes of the community present a wide variety of type. This sort of contrast can be found today at the pits. David Hewitson a public schoolboy from St. Bees and Bill Hibbs from Wigan."

Contemporary Newsreel

"They tell me you're a public schoolboy, it'll be a bit of a change for you going into the mine won't it?"

Conveyor tub transfer point - Ashington Pit, 1939.

"The war had been going on for three or four years and there was a tremendous need for ships. The Government decided for some reason to call up engineering apprentices, to send them down the mines. You had the crazy situation that instead of having been able to foresee the need for coal they had sent the miners away. And when they were desperate for coal they decided to call up, of all people, shipyard apprentices. The apprentices resisted that....There was no valid reason, no sensible reason, and so when the lads who were called up said, 'We'll go into the army but we're not going down the pits'.

It became a bitter battle. But we fought and appealed against the decision and won."

T. Dan Smith

"Tyneside's busy enough, but just remember what the yards looked like five years ago. Idle, empty, some of them derelict and the skilled men that worked in them scattered and forgotten. Will it be the same five years from now?"

HMS Anson, Sydney Harbour.

"During the war we built ships and we launched them. There was no pompous ceremony, we just launched them...during the war on the river Wear we were building something like three hundred thousand tons of ships a year....We didn't have time for ceremony. It seemed to me it was the efficient way."

George Hills, Wearside shipworker

Repair work being carried out at Smith's Dock, Middlesbrough, during the War.

100,000 North East women join the workforce.

"Although many new and important production methods are often introduced, the deft hands of women in filling factories are still the greatest factor in providing the fighting services with vital shell components in massive quantities."

Contemporary Newsreel

"As you can see the conditions are not likely to be particularly comfortable. You have to turn out at all hours of the day and night, in all sorts of weather conditions. You'll be half frozen, you'll bed your balloon in gales, you'll be ankle deep in mud, you'll be drenched with rain. If you get through this all right, as I know you will, you'll be ready for the worst site in the whole country. You may be in a town among people, I hope you will be, or by yourselves in the country. But either way the job is the same, and it's a vital one."

Barrage balloon instructor

A. T. S. - Autumn 1939.

"You are now a member. You are pledged to hold yourself available for service on the land for the period of the war. You have promised to abide by the conditions of training and employment of the women's land army. Its good name is in your hands, you have made the home fields your battlefield. Your country relies on your loyalty and welcomes your help."

Speech to Land Army recruits

Women's Land Army.

A Land Army hostel.

The nation pulls together to aid the war effort.

Children collect metal...

...factories are converted for military use...
The CWS cabinet factory at Pelaw making sections for Mosquito aircraft.

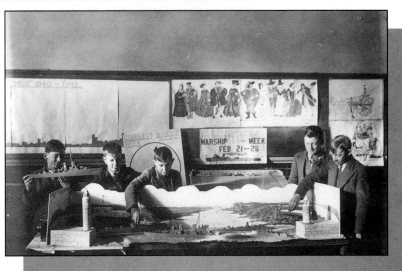

Consett warship week.

"Children from the council houses in Byker, Newcastle upon Tyne, are running a variety show to supply gumboots for the troops. The tops of Anderson shelters provide the gallery, and the ladies of the chorus step it out on a piece of carpet. Taking in the reserve seat bookings, that means ten and tuppence farthing for the troops. From the first house too - nice going."

Contemporary Newsreel

THE NORTH EAST AT WAR 1939-1945

The Royal Northumberland Fusiliers celebrate St. George's Day in Hexham (1939)... and in France (1940).

"I was very happy, quite honestly, to get out of the mundane job I was doing to get into a bit of excitement. I remember the first air raid siren going. We were sitting in a drill hall thinking there's not much protection if a bomb comes down - but then who was going to bomb Alnwick.

Going away from home was a big thing, even though it was not very far - first stop Amble, second stop Gosforth Park."

Colonel Bill Sanderson, RNF

An RNF reconnaissance motorcycle during the 'phoney war' in France.

Duke Killed Fighting In Flanders

THE Duke of Northumberland has been killed fighting

"All in all it was a fiasco. We can have all the tales we like about Dunkirk but to me it was a mess."

Fred Jameson

FOUR-FIFTHS OF B.E.F. HAVE BEEN SAVED

"We had been marching for days, fighting for days, we were nearly falling asleep as we moved. We landed in Dunkirk. It was the most amazing sight. You had to see it to believe it. It was a seafront just like Tynemouth - Black with troops."

RSM Martin McLane, DLI

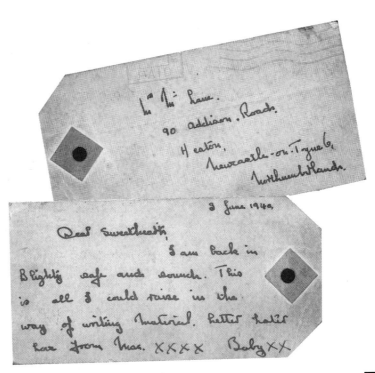

Squadrons formed in the North East fly south to join in the Battle for France...and then the Battle for Britain.

"I don't think any of us thought of it as the Battle of Britain at the time. I joined 607 Squadron Auxiliary Air Force at RAF Usworth simply because I wanted to fly aeroplanes. Hurricanes were very good aeroplanes. You could take quite a lot of bullets into a Hurricane before it collapsed. We were fighting over England which made a big difference. It was all over very quickly - you were up for only half an hour. You don't have much time to worry."

Wing Commander Joe Kayll

Many bombers fly from the airfields of North Yorkshire. Leeming... Linton on Ouse...Elvington... Dishforth...Topcliffe... Middleton St. George.

The Darlington Spitfire, bought with proceeds from a fund raising week.

69 MORE GERMAN PLANES SHOT DOWN
R.A.F. Lose 11
Fighters: Five Pilots Safe

"I flew Halifax aircraft. On some of the trips when they unveiled the board and you saw where you were going sometimes there was a lump at the back of your throat.

Normally you flew as a family - as a crew. Sadly after my seventh operation I lost that crew. We were on our way back from the target and we were attacked and hit pretty badly. We were set on fire. The navigator was slightly injured and the rest of us were alright.

But the aircraft was badly damaged. After we had been flying quite a while we expected the coast to come up. When it wasn't, and we were losing petrol, we got a fix - to our horror we were south of Paris. We had been flying on damaged instruments. We knew then that we would not get home. We cleared the coast by five or six miles. As we landed the skipper was killed."

Flt Lt Doug Finlay, RAF

HMS Kelly and her Captain, Lord Mountbatten, enjoy a special place in Tyneside hearts.

Lord Mountbatten.

"She was a small ship, destroyer, 250 men. Earl Mountbatten, Captain, a great skipper, we just loved him. Coming up the river was fantastic. I was on the ensign with a young lad from Sunderland, Geordie Hanlon, and our job was to raise and lower the ensign at every salute that was given coming up the river. All the factory hooters were going, all the ships sirens were blazing away. Any vantage point at all the people were there. A wonderful experience."

Ralph Scorer

HMS Kelly brought home for repairs.

"The first ship I noticed on my outside. Blew up with a hell of a noise. The second ship inside ahead of me, the same thing happened. When the third ship blew up I didn't wait any further. I rang double speed on the engines, turned towards the Commodore then straight ahead.

We left the convoy. Behind us was a scene of destruction, tankers burning, other ships sinking. We carried on till daylight until we met the destroyer. He asked where the convoy was. I said astern of us. He said wait for the convoy. Only half returned to the ships."

George Purvis

"Seeing all the ships together, it was great. However many times you could count the ships you always got a different number. I felt really proud to think that we had that many ships at sea at the same time."

Tommy Sanderson,
Bosun, Merchant Navy

30,000 merchant seamen lose their lives, 3,000 come from South Shields. No town loses more.

MR. CHURCHILL ANNOUNCES THE FALL OF SINGAPORE

Island Peace Signed in Ford Works

Call To The Nation
DISUNITY NOW WOULD BE MORTAL CRIME

The funeral of an RNF prisoner of war.

The fall of Singapore is the largest capitulation in British history ...85,000 surrender.

"The entire population was moved back into a very narrow peninsula around Singapore itself. The water supply was poisoned and there was dead bodies all over the place. That was one of the factors which caused the capitulation. On the 14th of February it turned very quiet and you sensed something was wrong.

On the 15th of February it was dead silence and then they came through, Samurai swords dangling and the rest of it. We were lucky because they went into the Queen Alexandria Hospital nursing section and that was where some of the worst atrocities were committed."

Fred Jameson

Food parcels being sent by the Green Howards.

Many men in the North East are held captive by the Japanese - many die. They are known as 'The Forgotten Army.'

*Hedley Verity and Norman Yardley,
Green Howards and Yorkshire and
England cricketers. India 1942.
Hedley Verity died in action.*

'An unknown English Soldier'.

*Green Howards
killed in
Norway, 1940.*

NORTH-EAST MEN FIRST INTO TOBRUK

The 50th Northumbrian Division sees more fighting than any other Infantry Division.

"I was carrying the colours. There was a sudden splat in front of me, I cast my eyes down and there was a rotten tomato splattered onto the road in front of me. I looked up and all the balconies had Arabs throwing rotten fruit down on us, obviously the GOC was right. The locals were getting uppity."

Colonel Bill Sanderson

DLI take a Mareth shower bath - crude but effective.

"None of the glamorous things got through. One ship did, it was loaded with hockey gear and that sort of thing. Nothing interesting like a packet of cigarettes or a bottle of whisky."

BRITISH HALT ROMMEL'S DASH FOR TOBRUK

Green Howards on the Mareth Line, 1943.

DLI trucks carrying infantry through a gap in an enemy minefield come under heavy shell fire.

RNF machine gunner carrying his Vickers up to a forward position in the hills near Salerno.

The capture of Cassino, now so battered it looks like a series of caves in the hillside.

An RNF mortar crew.

Operation Overlord. Allied troops land in vast numbers from man made ports into northern France. Northern regiments face some of the heaviest opposition.

Newcastle Journal
North Mail

ALLIES SEVERAL MILES INLAND
"Thoroughly satisfactory"—Premier

Royal Northumberland Fusiliers survey the aftermath of the battle for Caen .

Private W. Wheatley of 'A' Company, DLI 50th Division, in action from the ruins of a house in Douet.

Newcastle ⚜ Journal
North Mail
WEDNESDAY, MAY 9, 1945   A KEMSLEY NEWSPAPER

THIRD REICH 'DIED' AT MIDNIGHT

Jodl radios 'Cease fire'
And no sabotage

Everything Germany has is turned over to Allies

AT MIDNIGHT LAST NIGHT, WITH THE FORMAL "CEASE FIRE" ON ALL FRONTS, THE GERMAN THIRD REICH CEASED ITS LEGAL EXISTENCE AND ITS GOVERNMENT CEASED TO FUNCTION.

Crusade has reached its 'glorious end'

Total defeat. Hitler commits suicide in the Berlin bunker on 30th April 1945. Unconditional surrender is signed on the 7th May.

A quartet of Newcastle men on their way over the River Weser, Vicker's gun team Privates Evans, Bellamy, Burke and Deverson.

2nd Battalion, RNF. 18th April, 1945.

Field Marshal Montgomery about to receive the surrender of German Forces in North West Europe.

HIROSHIMA DISAPPEARED UNDER SMOKE CLOUD

Atom bomb raiders tell story of attack

WHAT had been the Japanese city of Hiroshima going about its business at 9.15 a.m. on Monday in the sunshine disappeared

> The Japanese surrender follows on September 2nd 1945.

The capture of a Japanese train by the DLI.

IT'S A LOVELY DAY TOMORROW 1945-1950.

Many people believe the end of World War II means a new beginning in Britain.

VE celebrations in Darlington and in Richmond (bottom).

The King, Queen and Churchill wave to the crowds gathered outside Buckingham Palace.

All over the North East people celebrate VE Day and the end of the war. Public holidays are declared...

Private Roberts of the RAOC tries a demob hat for size.

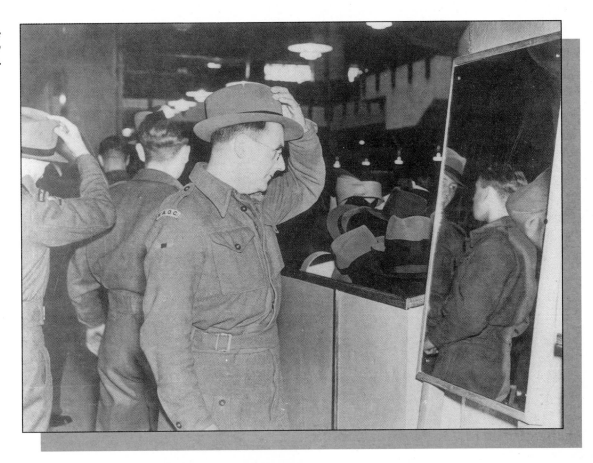

Troops from the Royal Northumberland Fusiliers meet French civilians at Dieppe, a woman offers 100 francs for some cigarettes and food.

Troops prepare to come home.

"We knew the people were going to change society if they could, and we knew that although Churchill was God he would be defeated.

When the war ended people really did say 'we're not going back to those years', and with all the difficulties that they faced, bad housing, bad schools, they made a tremendous effort."

T. Dan Smith

Temporary accommodation in the Church Hall at Kimblesworth, 1946.

A welfare state is promised. The North East is hopeful. There is a new mood of optimism, but for some...

"...then this officer put a notice on all railings. 'Married men without their own homes come to the ship's office and get these forms'. He dished them out to us and said 'fill these forms in and send it to your local council. If you don't fancy living in your home area then send it to that particular council and there will be a house waiting for you.' And we didn't think about it, although there hadn't been many houses built during the war - and anyway there'd been this firm knocking them all down. And there was an officer that had said 'send them in and you'll have a house', so that was it, we obeyed officers. Lying swine."

Sid France

Corrugated iron huts used by squatters at Chester-le-Street, 1946.

Railway carriages providing homes at Wheatley Hill, County Durham.

"When I was demobbed I went to Eston council. I was a bit surprised when the bloke said, 'there's going to be no house for you here kidda, you've been out of the area for six years.' And it was pointed out that I had been somewhere else and had been otherwise occupied."

Sid France

HOUSES SOON FOR EVERYONE

Mr. Bevan's promise to youth

"We heard about these camps being taken over... so I went down there and there was scads of people running round with furniture, kids and dogs and bumping into huts, I searched around and I finally found my little lass, big beaming smile on her face and she said 'Haway in here, this is our hut, we're in'.

It was half a hut about fourteen foot square, and there was an old bogey fire come washing stove at one end and nothing - no water, there were toilets but they were outside, the service toilets. And yet we did all right over the next few years."

Sid France

The first set of pre-fabs built at Consett, 1946.

41

BREAD TO BE DARKER STILL, & FEWER BISCUITS

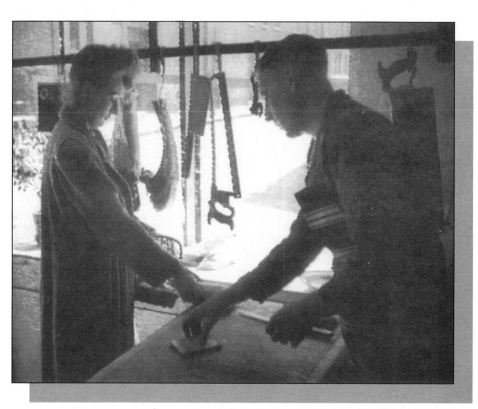

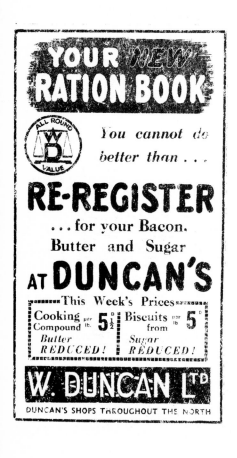

YOUR NEW RATION BOOK
You cannot do better than . . .
RE-REGISTER
. . . for your Bacon.
Butter and Sugar
AT DUNCAN'S
This Week's Prices
Cooking Compound per lb. 5½ᴰ | Biscuits per lb. from 5ᴰ
Butter REDUCED! | Sugar REDUCED!
W. DUNCAN Lᵀᴰ
DUNCAN'S SHOPS THROUGHOUT THE NORTH

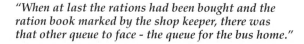

"When at last the rations had been bought and the ration book marked by the shop keeper, there was that other queue to face – the queue for the bus home."

"If there were any specials like shanks or anything that wasn't on ration, they used to have these big lists in the shops, you know from 'A' to 'W' and we were Webster and we were always at the end of the list. And that's why my mam had her ration books in two shops."

Evelyn Elliott

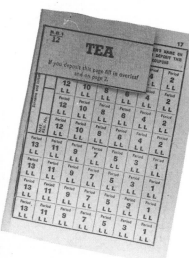

"From the beginning of 1948, the government will establish a State Register of doctors: all hospitals and specialist services are to be run by the State and a full health service, without fee, available to all."

Lord Beveridge

Lord Beveridge at his desk.

A large colony of pre-fabricated buildings is now being erected for the Ministry of Pensions at Newcastle. It will be from this centre that the new National Health scheme - popularly called the Beveridge Plan - will be directed.

"T.B. KILLS ONE A DAY IN NEWCASTLE"
Alderman denies "neglect" charge

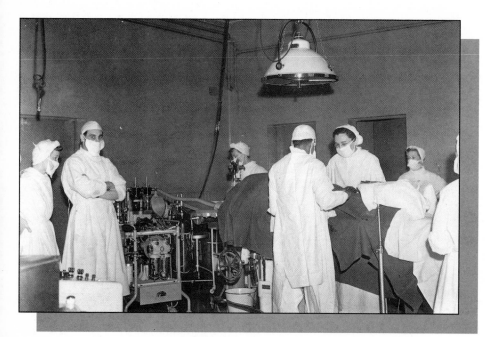

Dryburn Hospital, County Durham, 1948.

"A lot of people died prematurely from failure to attend a surgery or get a doctor in. Hospital beds also had to be paid for, the threat of anyone being ill was very worrying. The charities were very important prior to the N.H.S. because everyone depended on them, they sort of sank back a little into the distance. They were less important because the N.H.S. took care of everything. But as times get on we are now more and more depending on charities again."

Maureen Raper, SRN

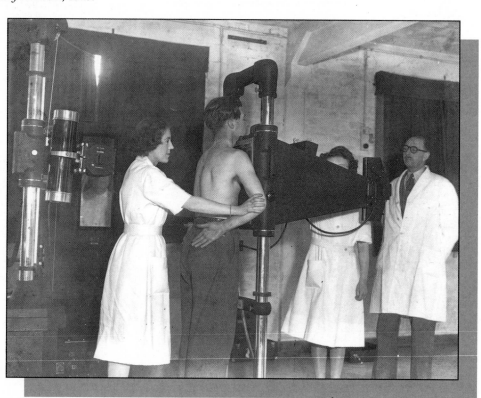

ATTLEE CALLS FOR 1940 SPIRIT IN INDUSTRY

"Harder work will bring prosperity"

"After the Second World War there is a new found prosperity in the North East. Order books are full and unemployment is at an all time low. The shipyards are busy replacing lost tonnage and production in the newly nationalised coal industry remains buoyant."

Swan Hunter's yard, Wallsend 1946

A busy Dunston Coal Staiths, just after the war.

"One of the things about nationalisation was that it took place at a time when there was a huge demand for coal. Industry was reconstructing generally in this country, coal was needed for that. Coal was a very valuable export and the government would have liked to have had as much coal as possible."

George Atkinson MBE, Head of North East Industrial Relations, NCB

Ships preparing to load at Dunston.

Coal and rail are the region's main employers. Their future is fundamental to the well-being of the North East.

Medomsley Colliery, County Durham, 1947.

"It upsets progress in terms of coal production, but it meant that coal had to be got anywhere it could be got, virtually coal at any price. Men were required to work in conditions in which they wouldn't be required to work now, and probably wouldn't work now. Very low seams - some as low as twelve to fifteen inches - working these seams by the old hand methods. Lying on their side with a pick and then shovelling it out, really very difficult. I don't think men would do it today."

George Atkinson

Drilling on a difficult face at Ashington Colliery.

"It was very dangerous. When you're down there with all that stuff on ya it makes ya wonder how it stays up. I saw one of my mates killed. It was nearly break-time. He was one of these lads that would work till the last breath. They would knock the compressor off, that was the signal it was bait time. He suddenly shouted, he shouted my name. He had a stone on top of him. He was barely marked. It just squashed the air out of him. It's a terrible experience."

Edwin Johnson, Durham Coal Miner

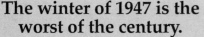

The winter of 1947 is the worst of the century.

"One of the things that upset the drive for more coal was the very severe winter that was encountered at the very beginning of 1947."

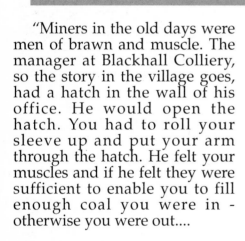

"Miners in the old days were men of brawn and muscle. The manager at Blackhall Colliery, so the story in the village goes, had a hatch in the wall of his office. He would open the hatch. You had to roll your sleeve up and put your arm through the hatch. He felt your muscles and if he felt they were sufficient to enable you to fill enough coal you were in - otherwise you were out....

Lifeboats out, sheep buried, in winter's first taste

BLIZZARDS AND GALES SWEEP COUNTRY

People collapse and die from intense cold

THE most severe spell of the winter—in which people died of intense cold — brought 60-mile gales and heavy snowfalls to various parts of the country yesterday.

Lifeboats had to put out to ships in trouble, farmers scaled frozen mountain slopes to dig out buried sheep, trees were blown down and roads were blocked by snowdrifts.

In the North and on Tyneside the weather was intensely cold but dry, and there was little interference with traffic.

"They're a grand body of chaps, they like their drink and their smoke but they work hard and they play hard, I think they did their best during the war, and I'm sure they'll do their best after the war."

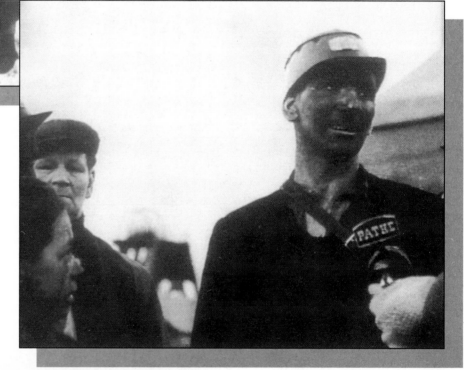

...For the miners, nationalisation was really something very hopeful. It meant the achievement of one of the long standing aspirations. It gave them hope that they would improve their working conditions and wages, and indeed this is exactly what happened."

George Atkinson.

Crook Drift Hole in the Wall Colliery marching at the miners' event of the year - the Durham Gala, 1949.

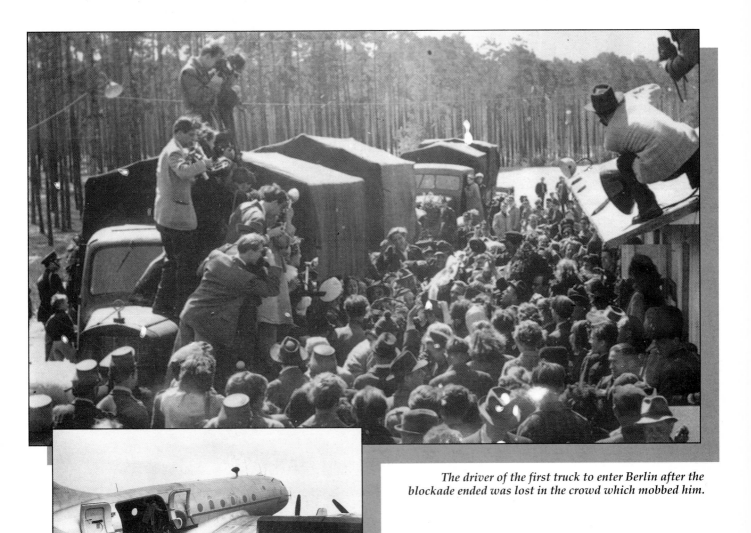

The driver of the first truck to enter Berlin after the blockade ended was lost in the crowd which mobbed him.

Berlin Airlift - a Dakota unloads 1949

British troops continue to see action abroad. The Green Howards embark at Suez for Malaya in 1949.

49

A future Monarch for a new age - Prince Charles is born.

"At Dawdon colliery, miners have built their own swimming pool and in their own spare time. The men had transformed the old weed covered pond into an up-to-date pool in just about four years. Later a bathing beauty display caused a bit of a stir and main interest was centred on twenty year old Eileen Hebson, Eileen was a real miner's dream."

Contemporary Newsreel

Prince Charles' christening December 1948.

Dawdon Colliery swimming gala.

The release from the pressures of war allowed people to go out and enjoy themselves once again.

Crimdon Holiday Camp, August 1946.

Women in tears as hushed crowd keeps vigil at Palace -
BRIGHT LIGHTS GO OUT

Churchill forms a new government in 1951. The King dies the following year.

The King's funeral cortege enters the Mall, February 1952.

CHURCHILL TAKES OVER
choose new Cabinet over weekend

EDEN, WOOLTON IN KEY POSTS

The Coronation takes place in June 1953.

Dr. Fisher, Archbishop of Canterbury, lowers the crown of St. Edmund onto the Queen's head.

Children listen to the Coronation at Shildon All Saints school.

Edmund Hillary and Sherpa Tensing relaxing after their climb up Mount Everest, 1953.

Coronation street parties at Darlington (left) and Durham (below).

STRAKERS LTD
Ford DEALERS
FOR REALLY RELIABLE
USED CARS
PHONE 21055

Newcastle Journal

North Mail — A KEMSLEY NEWSPAPER — 2d

No. 33,001 — SATURDAY, MAY 3, 1952

This will be a 20-years-after Cup Final clash with Arsenal at Wembley

1932-1951 **HERE WE ARE AGAIN**

"You thought you were transported into another world. I'd never seen Newcastle like this before. The first year we won the cup was the best. You could never repeat it.

It was a form of escapism. If a city or a town has a very successful football team a lot of people are a lot happier because it brings custom, it brings trade to the town. People have a better outlook and Newcastle certainly had it in those days."

Ray Raper,
United supporter since 1947

"The average gates for Newcastle were well in excess of 50,000. You had to get there half an hour before the kick off to get in. They frequently closed the gates twenty minutes or half an hour before the game started. It almost got to a form of religion.

With all the players on the same wages, around fifteen pounds a week, a couple of pounds bonus for a win, a pound for a draw - it fostered a better team spirit. That transmitted itself to the crowd. No violence, no obscene chanting, no segregation of supporters, it was a big family spirit really."

Ray Raper

The North's new towns are functional, low rise, spacious and clean. But they also charge higher rents and depend on the motor car.

From slums in Shildon to show houses in Chester-le-Street.

Newton Aycliffe is the first to be built.

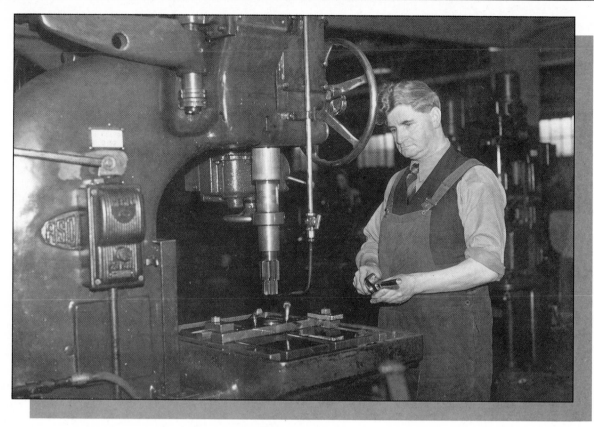

With new homes and shops comes new industry. The Newton Aycliffe Trading Estate, 1951.

New Town Blues

"It was just very attractive, although the building was very messy, dirty in parts. When we moved in it was a week before Christmas, the winter time, but it was something to look forward to, a house of your own in new surroundings.

From Shildon there was an hour and a half bus service - if you were lucky, and there were no phones.

The result was we got 'New Town Blues'. It was very real, it was very drastic. They would cry and cry and cry. They just did not know what to do."

Joyce Hardaker, moved to Newton Aycliffe 1952

Rescue workers emerge from the stricken pit.

"Easington colliery has suffered the worst mining disaster in County Durham for over forty years. Comrades and relatives of the entombed men are told hopes of rescuing them alive must be abandoned - the death toll is put at eighty."

Contemporary Newsreel

Local people anxiously wait for news.

North shipyards are leading world

TOTAL NEARLY HALF BRITAIN'S

Swan Hunter's yard, Wallsend.

"If the electronic impulse did not jump the trigger you had the emergency back up system - a fitter crouched in a foxhole with steel plate around him and a large hammer. If the trigger didn't go off he bobbed out of his foxhole , clouted the trigger to help release the last choke. The weight took over and he would crouch back down in his foxhole until the darn thing rumbled over his head into the Tyne...it could be quite exciting."

Ron French, shipyard worker

"There was fibre glass insulation being put into the holds of meat carrying ships, asbestos in the engine rooms. That was the sort of stuff inhaled without knowing the dangers at the time."

It's all coming to roost now with with people of 55 - 60 years old sliding away."

Ron French

Rivetting at Swan Hunter's. The man in the background is the catcher.

Consett works, 1955.

LADIES' SUN SUITS
25 6
66
F. Beavan, Ltd.

Newcastle Journal
North Mail
No. 12,685   FRIDAY APRIL 27 1951   A KEMSLEY NEWSPAPER

6 A.M.

GREAT FIGHT BY THE BRITISH

Losses heavy, but they smash Reds
R.N.F. HEROES

Fighting in the Korean war starts in September 1950. The DLI joins UN forces under American command.

The DLI (left) and the RNF (below) take a rest between patrols.

Dance Bands

"Everybody wanted to be a sort of Bing Crosby and the crooners in America and Britain were either high voice Crosbys or low voice Crosbys. I wanted to be a crooner like Crosby. The only way to get into that was join a dance band, every town had its assortment of dance bands. In my early days the lads and lasses would cheerfully do a rumba and the best one of all was the Bradford barn dance, because you got rid of your partner every twenty bars and there was some nice girls in those days ."

Frank Wappat

Jos Q. Atkinson, the leading society band leader. Resident at the Old Assembly Rooms, Newcastle, 1946 to 1958.

Labour lose the 1955 election.

Morgan Philips, Secretary of the Labour Party, with his new General Election Posters.

NEVER HAD IT SO GOOD 1955-1960

Lack of American support embarrasses Britain and France and sees a quick end to the hostilities in Eygpt.

Soldiers keep guard, as a ditched Centurion tank is recovered at the side of the Suez Canal.

Khrushchev and Eden.

Kas Ferrit in the Canal Zone. Service families shop at ramshackle shops with homely reminders.

First man in space - Major Yuri Gagarin.

Stalin's portrait is burned in Budapest's last battle for freedom.

Calder Hall, Britain's first nuclear plant. The top section of the reactor shell, was built by Whessoe of Darlington.

Newcastle United make it 3 FA cup wins in 5 years.

"It's ours again. That was the happy message on the engine which brought Newcastle United home with the cup. The civic reception at the station was followed by a tremendous reception from the people of Tyneside."

Newsreel commentary

Jimmy Scoular brandishes the cup.

Traffic problems.

"The policeman in Market Square has a closed circuit television system to give him a picture of traffic build-ups on two main approaches to the city. Situated on the Great North Road, traffic is one of Durham's greatest headaches, and this might be the cure - let's hope the copper doesn't get eye-strain."

Newsreel Commentary

Flowing smoothly in Durham City...

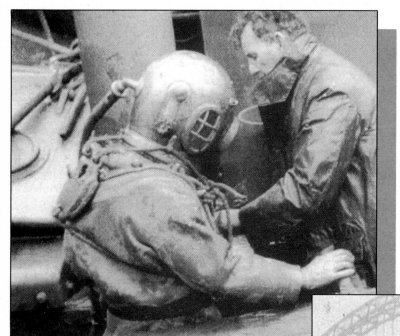

...but not so smoothly on the Tyne. Collier Cyprian Coast is refloated.

BATTLING TEDDY BOYS INVADE DANCE HALL

One, two, three o'clock...Rock and Roll

"This girl came up to me and said, 'Frankie will you play this one?' I said 'Is it a quick step or a foxtrot?' She said,'Divvent be daft man it's Rock Aroond the Clock.'"

Frank Wappat

Bill Haley and the Comets.

Elvis.

"With the advent of Rock and Roll, apart from the records and the strange form of dancing, groups of young people identified themselves to each town and village, and fighting became the hallmark of the day. The groups of lads from different areas would wear an emblem of some sort.

The most famous of all on the Tyne was a group from Daisy Hill, they wore a red carnation and were known as the 'Red Flower Gang'.

They paid me a visit in my dance hall. I was really delighted when I saw them coming up the street from the ferry, they looked particularly well dressed as if they were going to a wedding reception. In all there must have been a hundred of them in the hall that night. All was well, the Bradford barn dance was in full swing, when a whistle blew - of all things - and at that the hall erupted the hall was systematically wrecked."

Frank Wappat

Swinging in Spennymoor, 1955..

Lindisfarne Causeway and the great British summer.

"We'd set off at about about eight o'clock, and stop at the top of Newgate Hill, we'd have the usual romps that young people have and get on a coach and go to Filey, they would charge us one shilling and give us two meals. We saw various artists; Laurel and Hardy, Charlie Drake and Des O'Connor were Redcoats, we saw some very top line artists.

The secret of Butlins was that they had it all in bright colours, which is what people wanted to see after the war - all the greys and khakis. It just gave them an uplift. Just for that day they were in fairy land."

And to go on holiday you needed a car... The 1957 Motor Show.

"A car for him and another for her. His is a Zodiac and hers an Anglia. Bound to start an argument of course."

"It's an international show, which may account for the Ballet Rambert exercising their magic at the Renault stand."

"Or you may prefer a continental Bentley."

"Not 1/6, not a shilling, ladies and gentlemen - to you..." The traditional Sunday market on Newcastle Quayside.

Adult entertainment at the Hoppings.

New schools meet growing educational demands.

Durham Johnston School.

The Rex Cinema in Durham.

...as the television arrives.

TV showroom, 1957.

The Big Meeting.

"The Big Meeting they call it over here in County Durham. The one day of the year when the miners take over Durham City. Any pit that hasn't its own band hires one to escort the banner to the racecourse."

Newsreel Commentary

Everyone enters into the spirit on Gala Day.

Labour leader, Hugh Gaitskell addresses the Gala.

"You've never had it so good."

"Go to the industrial towns, or go to the farms, and you will see such a state of prosperity, as we have never had in my lifetime - nor indeed in the history of this country."
Harold Macmillan

Polio vaccination in Lanchester.

THE GOOD TIMES 1960-1965

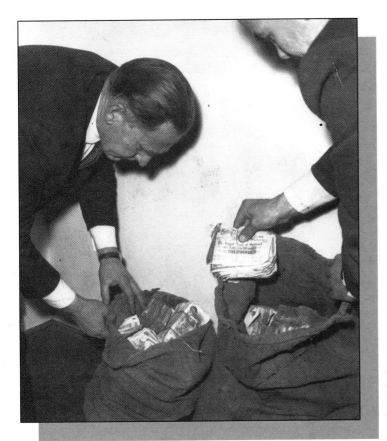

Police recover cash from the Great Train Robbery.

John F Kennedy.

Five years which saw the shooting of John F Kennedy, the erection of the Berlin Wall and, in Britain, the Great Train Robbery.

Memorials to some of those killed attempting to escape over the Berlin Wall - built in 1961.

"When we shut up shop in 1965 we were averaging, over the year, £15 a week, and paying well over £100 in wages. Trains were coming in and going out, nobody on them and nobody off them - depressing. We knew that when Beeching started - well we'd had it."

Ray Carr, Stationmaster at Staintondale

Locomotive production continues in the North for the time being - with a change from steam to diesel. The Darlington works finally stopped building engines in 1966.

The first main line diesel train, a Class 24, built in Darlington.

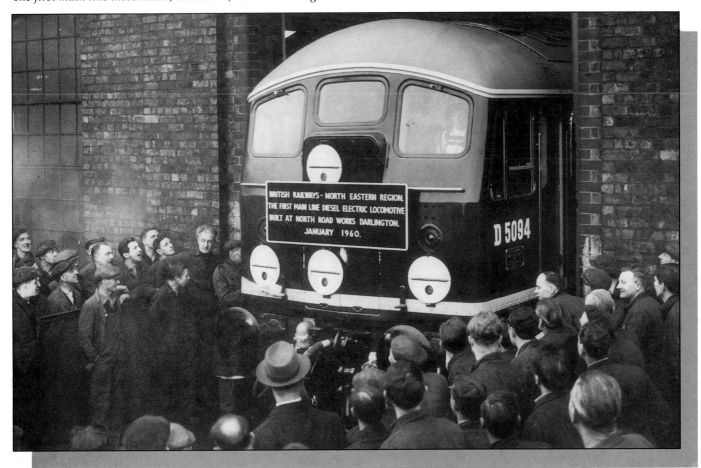

Despite foreign
competition the shipping
industry on the region's
three great rivers survives
intact.

*Three stages of ship construction
on the Wear.*

*An ore carrier arriving at
South Bank Wharf,
Middlesbrough.*

"No other shipbuilding town could do this."

Project 378, Wearside shipbuilders build a ship in a world record 9 weeks.

"We have the men, we have the equipment, we have the knowledge. We can build them one hundred and fifty thousand, one thousand, doesn't make any difference to us."

The Finnamore Meadow is launched on time.

Smiths join the great North Sea Gamble, launching their first oil rig. At Amble they still export coal the old way.

"There was plenty to cheer about as the first drilling rig in the 'North Sea Gamble' slid into the Tees. It had been built in seven months and the launch was only one year after the first tender. It was the first rig of this kind to be built in a British yard - and the first one anywhere to be launched like a ship."

Contemporary Newsreel

"It's getting into the food the children eat as well. The children are coming here red - their clothes and everything's just red. The children aren't getting any fresh air - and fresh air is a gift from God. Why can't we have it? Why can't Consett Iron Company be made to do something?"

Concerned mother

What do you wear in bed?
Perfume.
Nothing else?
A smile.

How much do you spend on a holiday?
Why, not a red cent.
Do you not have a holiday?
No.
Why not?
Because there's no need for a holiday, absolutely no need at all, life is extremely interesting, it doesn't matter where you are.

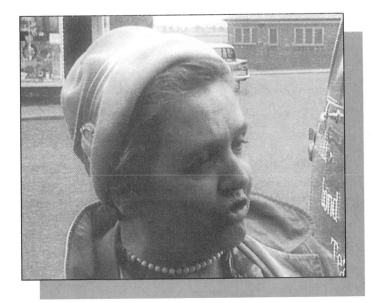

I think it's a ridiculous and unjustly thing, there's no heavy industry here for men. Do you think a man should go out from here and work all that time in travelling and coming back to have his dinner? Well, I think it's ridiculous.

Do you identify yourself with the characters you see in the adverts?
You know Miss Camay? The one who has the nice bath and everything - those bubbles. Well, I often think that could be me.

"The big talking point in today's newspapers is the exploding of the Rainbow Bomb over the Pacific. Russia says it was a crime, the newspapers say that it had to be done."

"Well I think it's a necessary evil. It's one of those things we don't like but we have to do it. I think it's necessary."

"I have to go and get the bath from the nail outside the wall, bring it into the house and if it was a heavy bath it's quite a hard job. I put it in the middle of the floor and fill it with cold water as far as it needs and I put the kettle on the fire and I put in kettle after kettle full until it reaches the right temperature then that child may have a bath."

"*This is what Mr Matthew Madison was paying 22/6 for. The room described at today's rent tribunal as 'little more than a lean-to in the rafters', is eight foot square, the only window is little more than a gap in the ceiling - it has no heating but there is an ageing cooker, said to be a fire danger. The decaying room that Mr Madison calls a home is one of two attics on top of a five room house. Seven families share one toilet, there is no hot water and the only bath is useless.*"

Building of New Towns continues apace.

"They had a vision that you could just have sunshine and light and you could make that a New Town. They were a great invention. They were things that were created, organisations that were created, where you were creating a community that wasn't just houses - but here were all the amenities and they could be created so that if you wanted to take population out of the overcrowded south east from London you could do that."

T. Dan Smith

£50m. NEW TOWN PLANNED FOR WASHINGTON

"The rents of the houses will be something in the region of £3 to £3 10 shillings per week - which of course includes rates - and actually people wouldn't get this type of home for this kind of money if it was private development."

"...the Corporation have really learnt from a number of mistakes in the past and are now really going places."
Richard Crossman

"Spacious, good family houses. I had a garden at the back, I had a small plot at the front, just a green, and they were very comfortable. For a lot of people moving from the old communities they were palaces."
Rita Jameson

91

"This is the last man only pub in a town where once they were the rule rather than the exception. It is a sad day for those of us who believe in a world of male superiority and a woman's place, or at least one of them, is at the kitchen sink or behind the bar, attending man's pleasure. But this is the last Christmas the pub will see before women are allowed in, here in Middlesbrough, a town of strong men and even stronger beer, a few of us have been fighting a rearguard action through the years.

The workingmen's clubs were the first to wilt under the feminine hammer blows and open their doors to wives and girlfriends and started to serve sweet fizzy drinks with foreign sounding names. Then the man only pubs started to go. But here in the Wellington you can find men with turn-ups to their trousers, men who like a short back and sides, a good swear in masculine company and beer with no froth on it.

The decision has been made to despoil this pub in a similar manner in 1966 - what then will happen to these fine men, whose wives have always been able to remain at home happy with the kids, the ironing and the polishing of the bosses boots ready for the next day?"

Tyne Tees Reporter

"When you've got a wife and kids to keep it doesn't make much difference at all. The money we're getting now we canna pay. We canna pay the rent, we can just manage to pay for food, we've got to go round neighbours for a bag of coal..."

An unemployed man on state benefit

The last 'men-only' bar in Middlsebrough.

Ya canna pay.

Signing on.

Newcastle's Animals top the charts with 'House of the Rising Sun.'

"My brother bought a record player, he was three years older than me and he bought records like Bill Haley, the Lonnie Donegan skiffle band, and I used to go round neighbours and watch the Six-Five Special which featured people like Lonnie Donegan and it just suddenly hit me and I thought I'd like to get a guitar."

Hilton Valentine

The Animals.

"This is it, the biggest social phenomenon of the 1960s. In three weeks time a bunch of long haired latter day minstrels called the Rolling Stones arrive here in the Newcastle, they're giving a concert, performance or whatever the proper name is for the frantic adolescent ritual of which they are high priests."

Tyne Tees Reporter

"What is their attraction? They act like clowns and you are prepared to buy a ticket to see animals like that. Do you think that if people come here with their banjos and hair down to their waists you can go and smash windows?"

THE AGE OF AQUARIUS 1965-1970

Five years when Russian Tanks were on the streets of Prague and students protested on the streets of London and Paris over the dragging Vietnam war.

Grosvenor Square, March 18th 1968, was the scene of violent demonstrations.

4 a.m. news

Russia invades sleeping Czechs

The Czech crisis, 1968.

Crumbling pitheap hits Welsh village

Houses engulfed— and farm disappears

Cordon holds back anguished mothers

Miners recalled to join rescue battle

160 CHILDREN MISSING AFTER LANDSLIDE BURIES SCHOOL

Winston Churchill dies in 1965.

There is racial tension as Enoch Powell makes his "rivers of blood" speech. Team Valley workers strike in support of his "freedom of speech"

Local lads Bobby and Jackie Charlton help England win the World Cup.

95

The Maharishi, spiritual guru of the rich and famous, including the Beatles.

"The Handyside Arcade, the Mecca of people in the North East who like to consider themselves 'with it.'"

Tyne Tees Reporter

"As men's hair gets longer and longer the favourite street game has changed from hopscotch to guess the sex of passers by."

Tyne Tees Reporter

The SS Ottawa nears completion .

Industry on the river Wear - coal staiths and oil tankers.

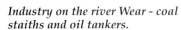

'The Ship at the End of the Street' The 90,000 ton Norwegian supertanker, Sir Winston Churchill, at Swan Hunter's yard in Wallsend.

North jobs gloom deepens

Tyneside factory to pay off 700 as three others announce closures

The last shift at Blyth Dry dock.

The Haverton Hill yard in Middlesbrough, with empty berths.

"Security people showed us round the canteen... I've been through some tunnels before, but I must say this is fantastic this one."

The first man through the Tyne Tunnel.

The new Scotswood road bridge under construction.

The trolley bus, last seen on Newcastle's streets in 1967.

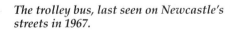

The Tyne Tunnel nears completion.

The Department of Transport introduces new measures to control growing traffic problems.

Barbara Castle, Labour Minister of Transport, anticipates the Metro: "The purpose of a conurbation transport authority is to improve the operation of public transport throughout the whole area... to develop a rapid transport system."

Lorry drivers in Middlesbrough try to prevent movement of goods into the town in a protest about the introduction of the "spy in the cab" - the tachograph.

Darlington becomes the home of the first woman traffic warden in Britain.

Mini pandas - the force takes receipt of its new fleet of police vehicles.

"I've got a Hotpoint washer but still I like to come down the washhouse...you can do an awful lot of clothes in 2 hours."

"I don't like being up a height... it's really lonely, when I go through the day I don't see anyone, there's not a sound. When you go in the house you seem as if you're locked in. I never sleep in it by myself."

"They tell you round here there's nothing wrong with a pawn shop - it's better than borrowing."

The remains of the Royal Arcade lie on waste ground in Shieldfield, Newcastle.

Swan House takes shape.

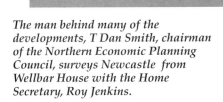

Sunderland also builds an extension to their art gallery.

The man behind many of the developments, T Dan Smith, chairman of the Northern Economic Planning Council, surveys Newcastle from Wellbar House with the Home Secretary, Roy Jenkins.

Newcastle Civic Centre under construction, 1968.

Bobby Moncur inspects the new addition to the silver ware.

Stan Anderson throws his shirt to the 60,000 crowd after the 2 - 0 victory over Bolton - the win that clinched promotion for Newcastle in 1965.

The international career of Colin Milburn, the 'Burnopfield Basher', is tragically ended in a motor accident in 1969.

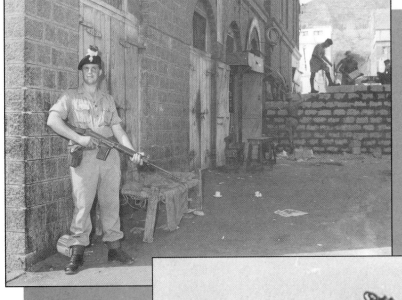

Fusilier Brian Merryweather from Blyth stands guard as a wall is constructed to prevent terrorist getaways.

An RNF check point.

Sergeants and NCO's at the last last dinner of the 'Fighting Fifth.'

"I never thought I'd see my only son lying in the gutters of an Aden street."

Mrs Vera Davidge

Army reorganisation signals the end of the 'Fighting Fifth' and the DLI in 1968.

The DLI is sent to Borneo in 1966 to combat communist insurgents.

The sand on Redcar beach mysteriously disappears.

Catherine Cookson visits Newcastle Quayside.

Local Art students discuss the finer points of their latest work.

"The purpose of art is basically visual communication and this is the problem which I have to face. The person has to know something about abstract art before he can begin to understand what I am trying to achieve."

THE TIMES ARE A CHANGING 1970-1975

The Sunderland Empire. Power failures become common during the 1972 coal strike.

Miners' leader Joe Gormley sees Ted Heath's announcement of a General Election.

The dustmen strike for £20 a week.

As the coal strike bites and electricity generation is severely restricted, industry operates on a three day week and every household stocks up with candles.
Further energy problems arise as OPEC flexes its muscles and dramatically increases oil prices.

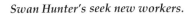

Swan Hunter's seek new workers.

Consett lies idle during the coal strike.

The nuclear industry is one of the few that experiences growth. The Seaton Carew power-station under construction.

A lonely walk for a miner crossing the picket lines at Easington Colliery in 1972.

Rows of netties in South Moor, County Durham.

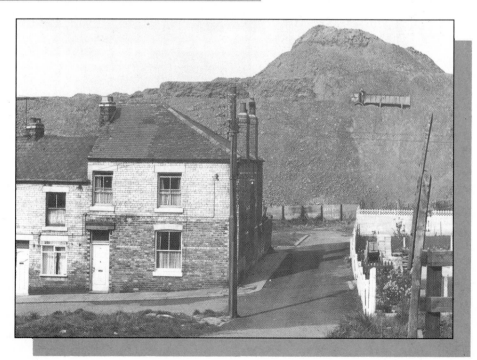

The Lingdale slag heap dwarfs the houses in the valley below.

Lindisfarne (note the causeway crossing time table behind them)

Glamour comes to pop music, although Newcastle's Lindisfarne stay true to life. Their album 'Fog on the Tyne' is number one in the charts.

Gary Glitter gets glam in 1974.

A skinhead is shown the door at Ayresome Park, Middlesbrough

A collection of missiles taken from people entering Roker Park, Sunderland, before a match.

"It's meant to have all started with Millwall back in the 60's, but that's just when the press got hold of it. I remember different crews fighting each other in the middle of the Leazes, and getting chased and attacked just because I had long hair. I gave up going in the end."

Jed Donovan, former Newcastle United Supporter.

The FA Cup comes to Sunderland in 1973 as they beat Leeds United 1-0, but Newcastle flop a year later against Liverpool. Gateshead's Brendan Foster triumphs in Europe.

"On the morning of the game, Grandstand told us that no team playing stripes had lost a cup final since the war. I just knew we were going to win."
David Brough (Newcastle go on to lose 3-0)

Brendan Foster won the 5000 metres European Championship at Rome in 1974.

A sharp-dressed Newcastle United squad visit the Oval in 1974.

"There was a fervour to get things done. Newcastle had been static. There had been very little done since the war and it had suffered from the depression before the war. There was great enthusiasm, there were enormous problems. It was a pioneering spirit."

John Stabler, Newcastle City Planning Dept.

One of the finest groups of buildings in the region, Old Eldon Square, is demolished.

"Whole Communities were ripped up, all the cosiness, all the social benefits of living in close communities was lost. Communities were torn apart and that was tragic."

Frank Atkinson, former director of Beamish Museum

"We brutalise our historic buildings with insensitive additions and alterations. We obliterate them in megalomaniac road schemes. We neglect them and demolish them and when the time comes to replace them we do it with buildings that are either plain ugly or nervously unexciting."

John Grundy, architectural historian

Newcastle centre in 1970, old buildings make way for tower blocks.

"The Great North Road ran up the middle of Northumberland Street. On the Saturday it was quite horrendous, with police horses keeping shoppers on the pavements. A lot of people might not like the form the road took. In fact it made an enormous difference to moving around the city."

John Stabler

The Great North Road flies over Gateshead.

The Central Motorway passes by Newcastle's Civic Centre.

Built in the mid-seventies to ease traffic congestion, the motorway is now one of the worst bottlenecks in the country as traffic piles up to cross the Tyne Bridge.

As motor transport becomes ever more popular, the decline in the railways continues. The Alston line is closed in 1975.

"Dozens of motorists who dipped into their pockets as usual for their store of parking meter sixpences got a nasty shock in Newcastle yesterday: the long stay meters had been converted to take shillings only."

Northern Echo

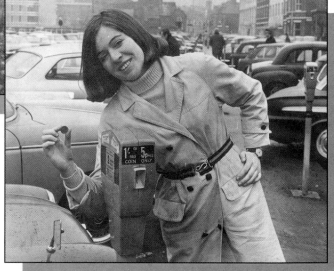

Street war in Belfast. The Green Howards complete tours of duty in Northern Ireland, and then join the waiting game in Minden, West Germany.

1st Battalion, The Green Howards, Northern Ireland, 1972.

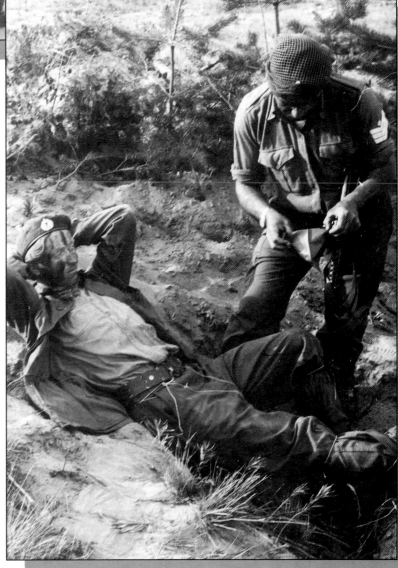

The rigours of war on the Rhineland plain, waiting for an enemy that never came.

THE WINTER OF DISCONTENT 1975-1980

An American helicopter lifts evacuees from a Saigon rooftop during the final days of the war

Vietnam finally draws to an ignominious close for the USA in 1975.

Mr Duc Tho (third from left) and Dr. Kissinger (third from right) with North Vietnamese and American delegates.

Sweat it out, say the weathermen

"We were urged to do all sorts of things to save water. You couldn't water the garden; you had to put a brick in the water cistern; sharing bathwater - most people preferred the idea of fitting a shower instead - which also served to save water."

Judith Evans, plumber.

Dennis Fletcher of Northumbrian Water - bewildered at diminishing water supplies at Derwent reservoir.

Trevor Marsay inspects the ground at Angrove Farm near Great Ayton in August 1976.

1977 proved to be a year of celebration with the Queen's Silver Jubilee, and Virginia Wade winning at Wimbledon.

That balcony again. The Queen's Silver Jubilee celebrations in 1977.

Virginia Wade prepares to meet the Queen after beating Betty Stove in the 1977 Wimbledon final.

In the same year Muhammad Ali makes a surprise visit to the North East to have his marriage blessed in a South Shields mosque.

The Queen in Newcastle during a Jubilee year visit to Tyneside.

Jimmy Carter is given the red carpet treatment as he arrives at Newcastle airport.

He later receives the Freedom of the City from the Mayor, outside the Civic Centre.

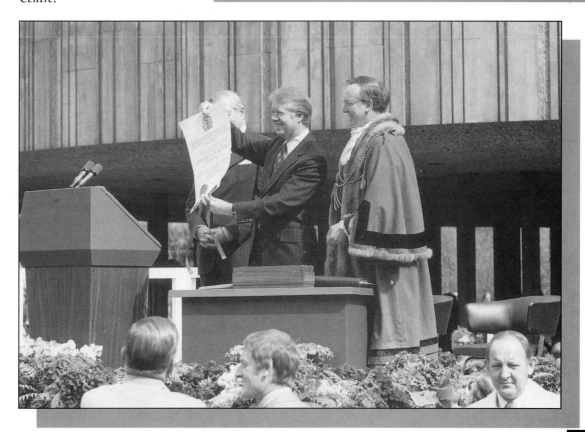

Forty one new stations are built for the new system. The Monument was one of four Newcastle stations built underground.

The outline of the proposed dam in 1970.

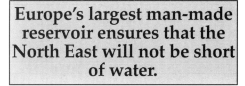

Europe's largest man-made reservoir ensures that the North East will not be short of water.

March 1982 inspecting the outlet pipe at Kielder dam.

George Geddes opens the dam in December 1980. The decline in heavy industry in the region meant that the dam has still to fulfil its intended role.

After his release from prison T Dan Smith has the opportunity to survey Eldon Square.

Newton Aycliffe has its own unique drive to attract industry.

"It took me just three days to come up with six smashers."
Estates Director Tony Cooper.

Newton Aycliffe Development Corp. is criticised for using a nude model, and a slogan "You don't need support in Newton Aycliffe" as part of its publicity campaign

THE JOURNAL

... NEWCASTLE UPON TYNE. TUESDAY JULY 27 1976 No. 40,467

Foster crushed by flying Finn

The North's sportsmen suffer glorious defeat.

Blyth Spartans progress to the sixth round of the FA Cup only to be knocked out by Wrexham in front of a capacity crowd at St. James' Park.

Newcastle are beaten 2-1 by Manchester City in the League Cup final, yet still return to a hero's welcome.

The late seventies sees the North East produce three famous rock stars.

*Chris Rea
from Middlesbrough.*

*Gordon Sumner,
Sting of the Police.*

Mark Knopfler of Dire Straits.

Punk becomes all the rage and the Sex Pistols set out to shock.

"It was great fun at the time, shocking all these people in the town. My only regret was having my nose pierced five times."

Edwin Brown, ex Durham punk

Mrs Barbara Ann Bibby who was disgusted with the language on the flip side of the Sex Pistols' Something Else single.

> **Fear is brought to local streets as a hoaxer points a finger at Sunderland as the home of the Yorkshire Ripper. The police narrowed the accent to four streets in Sunderland.**

"I'm Jack, I see you're still having no luck catching me...I'm not quite sure when I will strike again, but it will be definitely some time this year....Yours, Jack the Ripper."

The Ripper Tape

THE JOURNAL

NEWCASTLE UPON TYNE   WEDNESDAY, JUNE 27, 1979   No. 44,560   8p

Tape reveals that killer is Sunderland man

Ripper: Public Enemy No. 1

A letter above addressed to Mr Oldfield by the Ripper and below his signature and a postscript asking "Did you get letter I sent to Daily Mirror n Manchester?"

Det. Con. Young and Det. Sgt. Hammond with a copy of the tape played in pubs and clubs in Sunderland.

Historic day for Maggie

The advertising agency Saatchi and Saatchi's campaign is thought by many to win the 1979 election for the Conservatives.

LABOUR ISN'T WORKING.

UNEMPLOYMENT OFFICE

BRITAIN'S BETTER OFF WITH THE CONSERVATIVES.

Jim Callaghan at the 1979 Durham Miners' Gala.

Margaret Thatcher takes Office in 1979.

1984. The IRA's most ambitious attack at Brighton demolishes the Government's conference headquarters - but not the Cabinet.

1981. The World looked on at the wedding of the decade at St. Paul's Cathedral.

Division in the Labour party results in a split - leading to the formation of the SDP. Stockton MP and former Gang of Four member Bill Rodgers with Mick Thomas of Gateshead East in support.

Veteran Manny Shinwell, former Easington MP, returns to the Labour conference to harangue the rebels.

131

"I'd been on holiday and on the way back we called in on a friend. He took a bit of time coming to the door and said he had been listening to the debate in parliament. I was confused because parliament did not sit on a Saturday until he explained that we were at war with Argentina. That was the first I heard of it."

David Brough

Yomping became a byword for British determination and courage.

Argentinian surrender, Port Stanley.

The latest Ark Royal in the final stage of production at Swan Hunter's in Hebburn, during 1980.

Swan Hunter also built the new Sir Galahad - replacing the ship destroyed at Bluff Cove.

Many people, objecting to the appointment of such an outspoken, anti-establishment figure as David Jenkins as Bishop of Durham, saw the subsequent fire at York Minster following a lightning strike as a judgement from on high.

Undeterred, Jenkins continued to speak his mind on a wide range of social issues as well as questioning some of the fundamental tenets of Christianity

Basil Hume, from Newcastle, became leader of the Catholic Church in Britain.

Tyneside celebrates.

The Queen officially opens the Metro in 1981.

In 1980 Newcastle celebrated 900 years since its foundation.

Brendan Foster congratulates crutch competitor Harry McClure after finishing the 1981 race.

Europe's biggest road race comes to the Great North.

Steve Cram, the Jarrow world record breaker competes in the Newcastle Road Race.

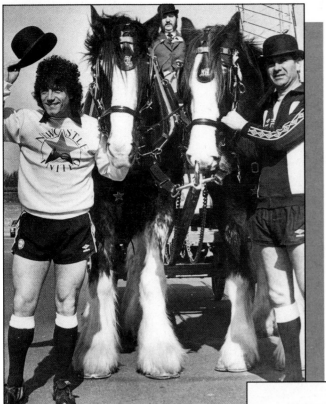

The Messiahs arrive at Newcastle and Sunderland - but Middlesbrough are on the brink of extinction.

"Nobody could have believed the ill fortune which McMenemy brought with him. The club was relegated to the Third Division for the first time in their history."

Jez Robinson

Lawrie McMenemy arrives at Roker in 1985.

Captain Kevin Keegan, with manager Arthur Cox (the ones on the outside) with Newcastle's new mascots. Keegan was embraced by Tyneside. Local genealogists even managed to find evidence that Keegan was a Geordie.

Financial troubles at Ayresome threaten the end of a great club.

The family dispute. Local Miners march on London.

"It seems to me ironic that there are people of my generation who as young men and boys were conscripted into the coal industry - told it was vitally important for the nation, and the nation says they must work there. Years later, when they are getting on in life - because of the decline in the industry a redundancy situation arises and they are told 'sorry, you ain't wanted any more'"

George Atkinson

Easington pit, 1984.

138

"The declining number of pits came about because of increased competition from other fuels and the importation of foreign coal at very cheap prices. It knocked the industry severely in this country and particularly Northumberland and Durham.

Another factor was industrial relations which have unfortunately declined in recent years, some people say that the great strike of 1984 made things worse in terms of the decline of the industry. Others would say it was inevitable - it would seem to be coming anyway."

George Atkinson

Miners digging for coal along the Hawthorn mineral line in County Durham.

The home of a coalboard storekeeper daubed by pickets.

The end of a way of life in Middlesbrough - Smith's dock closes.

Smith's Dock workers march on Middlesbrough.

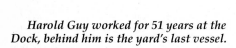

Harold Guy worked for 51 years at the Dock, behind him is the yard's last vessel.

Japanese investment brings many jobs back to the region.

British Steel, Consett, 1981.

Far East meets North East, Charlie Spedding enjoying katsu whilst the director Toshiniko Sekane tucks into roast Beef in Nissan's canteen.

141

Picture Acknowledgements

The publishers would like to thank the following people and organisations for the use of their pictures:

Swan Hunter's p. 16, 28, 61 (top), 62 (top), 98 (bottom), 133.

Newcastle Central Library   p.73 (left), 74 (bottom), 116 (bottom).

Newcastle City Engineers   p.121, 135.

Tyne and Wear PTE   p.121, 122.

Middlesbrough Library   p.17.

Cleveland Archives   p.10.

British Steel plc   p.82 (top left).

Saatchi and Saatchi Advertising   p.129 (top).

Darlington Library   p.26 (centre), 38 (centre), 54 (top).

Durham Archives   p.82.

Ray Carr   p.13 (centre).

Jean White   p.20.

Mr & Mrs Ruddy   p.70 (right).   Sunderland Echo p. 9 (top)

Durham Light Infantry Museum   p.32, 35 (centre), 37, 68, 106 (centre).

Green Howards Museum   p.30, 31, 34, 36 (top), 38 (bottom), 49 (bottom), 63, 81 (bottom), 117.

Royal Northumberland Fusiliers Museum   p.23 (top & centre), 34, 35, 36 (top), 38 (bottom), 49 (bottom), 63, 81 (bottom), 117.

Northern Echo   p.9 (top), 20 (bottom), 62 (top & bottom), 64 (middle), 66 (bottom), 82 (right), 87 (top left), 88 (top left), 89 (bottom), 90 (bottom), 91, 98 (centre), 102, 103, 104 (top), 107 (top), 108 (top left), 109, 110 (top & bottom), 111, 112, 113 (centre), 114 - 116, 119, 123 - 128, 129 (centre), 131 (left), 134, 136 - 141.

Beamish Museum   p.7 (bottom right), 8, 11 (bottom), 11 (top & bottom), 12 (top & bottom), 14, 15 (bottom), 21, 39 (top), 40, 41, 42 (bottom right), 44, 45 (bottom), 46 (top & bottom), 47 (bottom), 48 (bottom), 51, 53 (centre), 54 (bottom), 57 - 59, 60 (bottom), 61 (bottom), 69 (bottom), 72, 77, 86 (top right & bottom), 88 (bottom), 97 (bottom), 98 (bottom), 99 (top & bottom right), 110 (centre).

The Hulton Picture Collection   p.29, 43 (bottom), 49 (top & centre), 50 (top), 53 (top), 64 (bottom), 65 (top & bottom left), 66 (top right), 78 (bottom), 93 (bottom), 94 (centre & bottom), 95, 118, 120 (top & centre), 129 (bottom left), 130, 131 (top right).

Middlesbrough Evening Gazette p. 10 (bottom)

All other photographs are copyright of Pathe, Movietone, Imperial War Museum and Tyne Tees Television.